This book is dedicated to my son Brandon, his wife Donna, and my beautiful grandchildren; Brandon Jr., Alyssa, Christina, Rita, AJ, Lola and Olivia.

May you never forget your heritage nor your culture. May you understand the blessing of being bilingual. And may you always be Boricua proud.

I would also like to acknowledge the grandmothers and great grandmothers who love their babies unconditionally. My mother Rita has given so much of herself in both the raising of my son, and taking care of every one of her great grandchildren. My love grew for her, because of this selflessness, and all of my childhood distress disappeared. It is triple the love, she would often say. This book is also for her.

Mamabuela was born in San Juan, Puerto Rico, in 1901 according to her registration. I found a lot of her information on-line and surprisingly it all matched the many stories that she entertained me with, as a child.

Her father is listed as 100% Taino, a Caribbean Arawak native, who somehow survived genocide. I now know that many did, in spite of the false history fed to us. He was a pharmacist, according to the documentation, but Mamabuela referred to him as a healer. His registered name was Jose and he was related to Güeybaná, who was also known as Agüeybaná El Bravo.

Mamabuela's mother was directly from Spain. Her name was Josefina. There is reference to her having Armenian blood too, but I could not trace it back. Her registration was very formal as one would expect. I can only imagine that my great grandparents love and marriage was quite controversial for that time. That they overcame it all and lived a life of wealth and abundance is testament to our innate perseverance as Puerto Rican's. It is also a family trait.

Statue of Agüeybaná II, " El Bravo", in Ponce, Puerto

San Juan, Puerto Rico.
Circa 1901.

As was customary for young girls of that time, Mamabuela received a fifth grade education before she was pulled out of school. Her family was wealthy and she told me many stories about her lonely childhood in spite of having a sibling, her brother Rafael. She was groomed to simply enjoy the abundance ,and be pampered, until a proper suitor came along. My grandfather did sweep her off of her feet to continue a life of servants and opulence.

When they divorced she moved to New York, leaving it all behind. The marriage had become abusive and loveless. She invested her wealth in her brother who became Puerto Rico's first film and movie mogul, of that time.

I was blessed to be able to enjoy my great uncle's theater in New York, thanks to Mamabuela's investment. She took me to the many concerts and movies that shown at "El Teatro Puerto Rico". My great uncle had not only built and operated all of the islands movie theaters but had brought two to the big city.

We also visited La Tapia, his theater in Brooklyn. It was close to home. She immersed me in my culture. The music, the Spanish speaking movies, and even meeting some of the islands famous. I loved being Latina, thanks to Mamabuela.

Looking back now, and I suppose the true purpose of this writing, is not to tell Mamabuela's story in detail but to share her wisdom. A wisdom that was not only unique to her, a woman with a fifth grade education, but is also Puerto Rican grandmothers in general. I could go on and on to tell her story. It is truly one of strength and incredible kindness.

Most notable, to me at least, is that when she passed away, thousands of people attended her funeral. This tiny woman from an equally tiny island had made such a huge impact on so many lives.

It was her pride for her culture. She sang *En mi Viejo San Juan* constantly. When I asked her if she knew another song she once answered "I pray these lyrics, I'm not singing." Her many Puerto Rican friends and acquaintances loved being around someone so truly in love with her people.

It was also her goodness. She attended every religious gathering that she could. It did not matter whether it was Catholic, Muslim, Pentecostal, or even Jewish. She was often invited to speak. And she always gave to their causes. She said it was her calling.

The late, great, poet and author, Maya Angelou, once wrote "The desire to reach for the stars is ambitious. The desire to reach hearts is wise." This was the wisdom of Mamabuela. She reached so many hearts, including mine.

So many years since she has passed and I can still hear her "refranes". This is the Spanish word for cultural sayings. She barraged her family with them. I was often annoyed with hearing them over and over again, along with her explanations or lessons.

Today, in this writing, I crave to share some of them with you. Specifically the refranes that I hold near and dear to my heart because I've had to refer back to them as an adult. Some have even saved my life. I have read that you are what you think. If so, my Grandmother's sayings, deeply embedded in my psyche, are all that I am.

She used to say that the coqui, a loud but tiny frog that is indigenous to Puerto Rico, demanded to be heard and that I should too. It is her wisdom that demands to be heard.

This means pick your battles. You're not always the one holding the shotgun. You are human, and often wrong, and no more than a bird in someones site. Or, your being right is not as important as the person your battling with. Why kill the bird and the relationship.

I grasped this one late in life. Now being right is not as important as being kind. People respond to kindness and I feel better about myself.

Spanish

El pajaro tirandole a la escopeta

English

The bird firing the shotgun

Spanish

Dios aprieta pero no ahoga.

English

God will choke you but he will not kill you

There will be many times in your existence when you will feel the stress of life. It may be that the universe is providing a lesson. It may also just be a normal part of adulting.

Don't over think or over worry. Neither will provide a solution.

Always refer to the last monumental issue that you survived.

Learn from each mistake so that you don't repeat them.

Don't be too proud to ask for help.

This too shall pass.

Smile in the face of adversity.

This is a play on Spanish words and a simple life lesson.

Don't change the depth of your rock bottom. We are designed, as thinking beings, to rise above the worst of our circumstances.

Perhaps the lesson was to live simpler, or within your means, but never below your standards.

Don't ever take advice from anyone who is more screwed up than you are or who has a history of issues.

Remember too that your very worst situation is someones dream or goal. Keep it real and your perspective healthy.

Spanish

Saliste de Guatemala y te metiste en Guatapeor.

English

You have gone from bad to worse

Spanish

Olvídate, más se perdió en la guerra.

English

More was lost in the war. Forget about it.

You will lose the most precious of inanimate objects over time. No thing is permanent. Don't become a seeker or lover of things when people or your memories of them are more important.

As I write this page I realize that I am living this lesson from Mamabuela. Her sayings and her lessons are what I share with you. She left me nothing of worldly value but her love of life, her family, and her island are truly invaluable.

Collect the love. Remember the good times. Cherish the memories

Mamabuela was a Santera. One of the highest known in New York at her time.

Santeria is an Afro-American religion of Yoruba origin that originated in Cuba among West African descendants and made its way to Puerto Rico. *Santería* is a Spanish word that means the "worship of saints". It is influenced by Roman Catholicism and every Saint has a Santeria equivalent persona. Some, who don't understand it, call it voodoo. Mamabuela never did anything evil with her powers. Instead, it was her Zen, and how she dealt with life issues. The nature of Santeria made the Saints more relatable or accessible. She would pray to them and if they failed her, she would punish them. This punishment ranged between turning their statues on their head to not leaving them goodies on her altar. One statue, in particular, would get the brunt of her anger. It was her Indio; a native who she spoke to often. Perhaps it depicted the spirit of her father. Although she tried to pass her Santeria baton on to me, I never embraced this tradition. Her point with this saying was to say that even saints are not infallible.

Be gentle with yourself. You are neither a sinner nor a saint, just human. When you come to know better, you do better, but don't let mistakes be a life sentence.

Spanish

A cada santo le llega su día.

English

Every saint has their day.

Spanish

Una sonrisa no cuesta nada pero vale mucho.

English

A smile costs nothing but has great value.

Mamabuela was known for two physical attributes, her beautiful legs and that she was always smiling.

"It starts my day properly." she would say while having me practice my smile in the mirror.

I still practice my smile every morning and have done so on the most difficult of days.

Not only does your smile help you to feel better but it is your gift to your family, friends, and people who need your sunshine.

It introduces you even before you say a word.

Mamabuela also said that although Puerto Ricans come in all different shades, all different colours, and all different backgrounds, it is our smile that unites us. She said we carry the island in our smiles even if we have never been set foot on its shores.

I leave you with her morning words, translated to English:

Show some teeth and share your happy!

One of life's greatest forces is gratitude. Finding time to express who and what you're grateful for will change your life. It has mine. To be completely honest, I did not understand this particular 'refran' (saying), until I embraced the true meaning of gratitude.

We are so busy wishing we had instead of appreciating what has been given to us in many shapes or forms.

We've become a society of too much and wanting more, instead of thank you.

The universe will gift you the "driving" once you express your gratitude to everyone who has given you a "ride".

It is not weak or feeble, to be consistently thankful. Start with being grateful for another day and another chance to make someone smile.

Enjoy this ride called life.

Spanish

Te doy pon y quieres guiar.

English

I give you a ride and you want to drive.

Spanish

Díme con quien andas y te diré quién eres.

English

Tell me who your friends are and I'll tell you who you are.

For all my Puerto Ricans:

"We are survivors", Mamabuela would always say. We are of strong black African blood, those who endured slavery for far too long. We are the Taino, a welcoming nation of Caribbean natives whose land and women were raped and pillaged. And we are also our oppressors, the Spanish conquistadors of that time, who did not know any better. It is this fierce combination that we must always be grateful for, in its entirety, because it is our make up. Boricua proud isn't just another refran or saying. Think about the chances of this tiny island, only 100 miles by 35 miles, and its people surviving not just this history but its many hurricanes & earthquakes, all of these years. As you ponder this history and Mamabuela's teachings, choose your tribe wisely.

For everyone:

Your friends should be a part of a better you, and you a better them. While you should always love unconditionally, don't mistake those words as an excuse for accepting toxic relationships.

If you're the smartest person in the room, you are in the wrong room. Align yourself with human beings who challenge your brain, your heart, and your kindness. Seek to understand and not just to be understood. And always, always, always bring value and seek value tin any relationship. That has nothing to do with money, by the way.

Spanish

Mañana será otro día.

English

Tomorrow is another day.

When Mamabuela passed away, I was broken. I didn't fully understand the effect losing her would have on my life. I struggled in many of the aspects that I have shared herein, and I speak not only from her lessons, but from experience.

Abuela means Grandmother in Spanish, but I called her Mamabuela, giving her the power in my life that she deserved from a very young age. She was both my Grandma and a second Mother. So you can imagine that the loss was twice the pain. I am grateful for her wisdom and that I was blessed to internalize it. I am thankful for all of the time and conversations we had. I am a proud Latina and Boricua, thanks to her.

Now that I know better in life, I do better, and most importantly I practice what she preached. She left me with twice the love, as many Mamabuela's do.

Lightning Source UK Ltd.
Milton Keynes UK
UKRC010101240120
357520UK00005B/92